THE OVERFILLED CAGE

POETRY FROM MY HEART

JAYAK CHATTERJEE

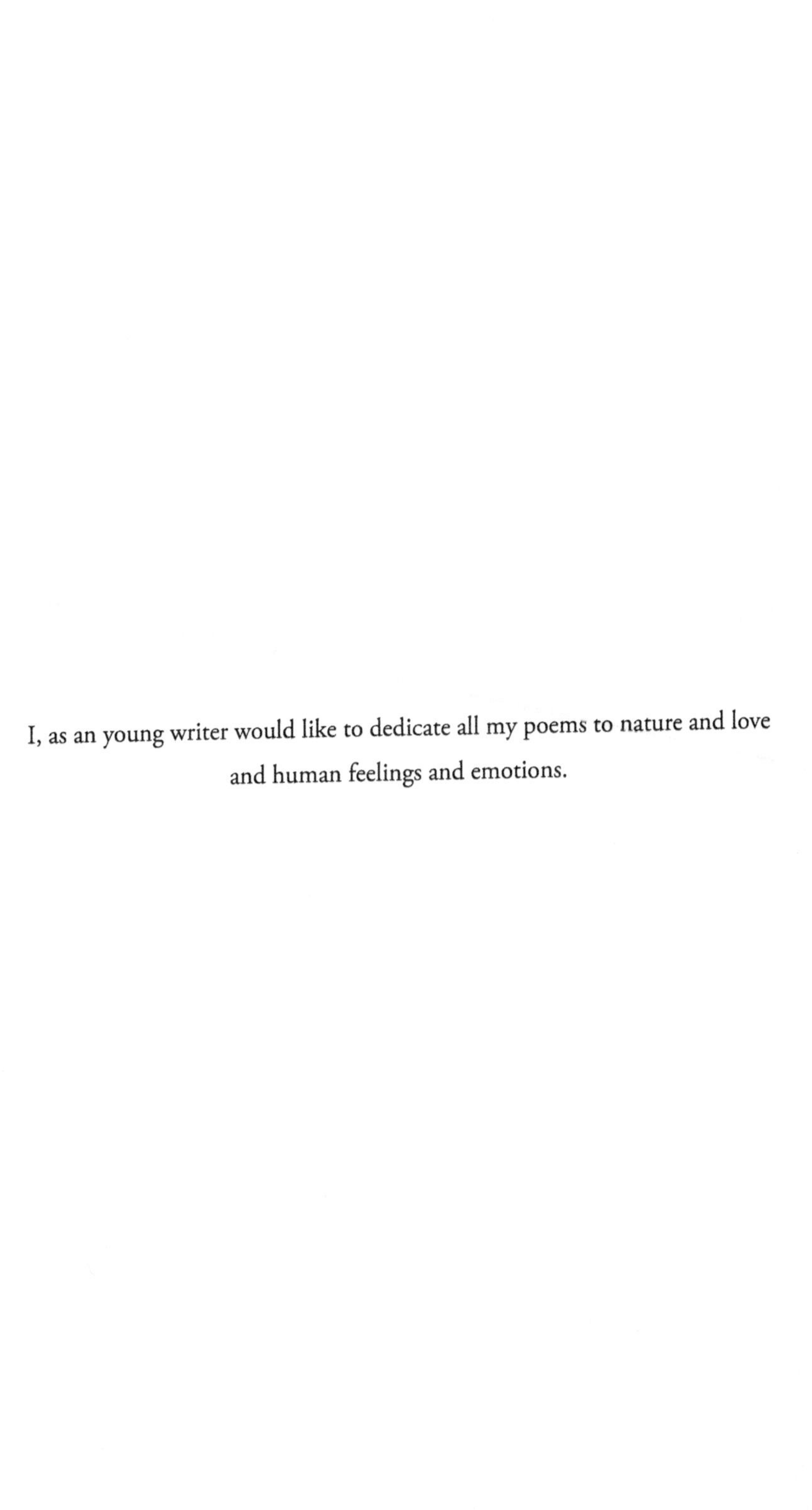

I, as an young writer would like to dedicate all my poems to nature and love
and human feelings and emotions.

Contents

Preface

I am Jayak Chatterjee, a student of Delhi Public School Joka(South Kolkata), and I am currently in 10th standard. I started poetry writing in class 8 and I remember that I started it just for fun. Slowly as time past and I grew, I realized that all the poems I write is so naturally coming and soon I found poetry as a way of expressing my emotions.

Acknowledgements

I acknowledge my parents, my mother Rupnanda Chatterjee, my father Anish Chatterjee, my sincere english teacher Mr. Archisman Sarkar who made me capable to write today. They all helped me and guided me all my life and as a result, I have reached this position that I can confidently write with fluency.

Index

Foreword

I being a 16 year old student, realized that in our generation, literature is fading away. We need to preserve our culture and enrich it. In order to do that we must not lose touch with literature. I strongly feel that in this digital world, people need to understand the importance of literature and art. To express all these concerns, this book contains 6 of my poems.

Prologue

"Poets express their emotions not through their face but by through their
pen."
This book contains poems on human emotions, sorrow, grief, love and
life.
"More than debates and practices, culture is expressed by texts and
writings."
"A writer's best friend is a pen, he cries through it and smiles through
it."

1. The Golden Feeling

I met her and it was true,
The feeling i had for her was truly what I desired.
Even though it might hurt, I never got tired.
I knew the whole thing was risky,
I gave it a thought, even though I wasn't frisky.
I realized that it was pure,
I gave it my best try even though I wasn't sure.
We were in a moment,
Knowing it might turn into a torment.
I feared that if I said it might be the end.
Still I said it with all intend.
That was the last I saw her,
My feelings remained the same, as pure as gold.
Perhaps I knew it could never get old.
It didn't make me weak, it gave me strength
That was the power of love I took till my end.

2. The Fiend

When you feel unworthy for life,
I will be there by your side.
When nothing is right,
And you are disgusted by your own sight,
I will stand by your side,
Laughing at you but I won't fight.
Like a catalyst in a reaction,
I will only trigger your action.
Afterall my ultimate goal is your happiness destruction.
When you are happy,
I will wait for you to be sad.
Because my hunger will suffice,
After eating everything you had.
Only love can save you from me,
Only it has the power to enrich you.
But since I am by your side,
I know love has already betrayed you.
I am depression, your eternal friend,
And I know, I always will be.
I am a dent in your soul, which you can't mend.
And that's how sad is your life, you see !

3. Winds Of Life

Like the way the wind blows,
My life goes in that flow.
It faces so many obstructions,
Still it keeps going without hesitation.
Winds never stopped,
Nor did my life.
It keeps going,
Even if the way is blocked.
Winds flow, and it bends
So does my life.
The winds bend for good.
But my life bends not the way it should.

4. The Fallen One

I was so sad and depressed in the beginning,
I was weak, fragile and bullied soul.
For me all these were ground shaking.
I had no choice but to accept it all,
But this time I knew I couldn't fall.
So I made my choices and decisions.
I made my options with a lot of precision.
I was really successful,
The feeling was great and it was actually wonderful.
I rose up quickly and swiftly,
And in no time I was in my prime.
Like Morningstar, I did really shine,
With all that prestige and pride,
I never really needed anyone to confide.
I was so confident and proud
It all made me feel like a light bringer.
Until they stung me like a freaking stinger.
For the first time I doubted, could I really win?
Oh! Let me tell you it wasn't really fun,
Cause now it made me the fallen one.

5. Being Evil Has A Price

My deeds aren't right,
Still I don't fight to make it.
I accept all of my sins.
It doesn't matter how much I try to be clean.
I got a nasty reputation,
Whatever I do is the worst combination.
I get many dirty little secrets,
Tell me yours and I will keep it.
Do you really want to know my name,
Cause if you don't its a shame.
Its written in golden glory and flame
But before asking me my name,
You better think twice,
Cause being evil has a price.
You won't know
Because you are just fine.
Perhaps you know, you can't ever shine.
So you better think twice,
Cause Being Evil Has A Price !

6. Curiosity Kills A Cat

I met a man who was very curious.
I asked him why he was so anxious.
He said because he wants to know eveverything,
I asked why
He said because I am a dizzy guy.
I said he was so daring,
He said because he ain't fearing.
I said it will cause you pain,
He replied, "You are so stupid, your words will go in vein"
I said you have a bad demeanour.
He said, "You are worth a peny, you are so cruel"
I said your curiosity will make you suffer and pain
Followed by eternal rain.

Conclusion

Atlast I would like to conclude on this note that many more poetries are yet to come from my side and hence many more books. Also I would like to thank all of my friends, family members, teachers and especially my mother, father and my english tutor for my path to success. I would like to thank them all for enriching my life and giving me the best education.